ALEX BALPHH
HUNTER FREEMAN
KENDALL WERNET

MASTERING
A Career Fair

A SIMPLE AND DIRECT GUIDE FOR LANDING YOUR FIRST JOB OUT OF COLLEGE

Mastering a Career Fair
A Simple and Direct Guide for Landing
Your First Job Out of College

Printed in the United States of America

First Printing, 2014

ISBN 9781507602843

In memory of our best friend, Kendall A. Wernet.

You put your heart and soul into this book.

We will never forget the impact you had on our lives.

– Alex Dalpiaz and Hunter Freeman

"A boring life is a wasted life."

– Kendall Wernet

CONTENTS

WHO IS THIS BOOK FOR?

Nothing greater is on the forefront of a graduating student's mind than obtaining that perfect job. When it comes time to graduate from college, the majority of society will emphasize the importance of "facing the real world."

Your mother and father probably cannot wait to see their baby bird depart from their nest. More than likely, you don't want to live there either because you have a world to explore! Perhaps the thought of being viewed as a failure by your peers due to your lack of employment has you worried. Not to mention that you may have thousands of dollars of debt piled up from your years of school. If you agree with any of these thoughts, then this book is for you.

It was at this very point of realization, panic, and

desperation that this book was conceptualized. We wanted to provide a resource of hope and guidance to anyone striving to overcome the overwhelming job search. This book will take you on an explicit journey to help you master some very important steps to increase your chances of landing that job. In this book, we cover three vital stages you must master to succeed in your job search:

1. **We show you how to master a career fair and uncover a proven method that less than 1% of candidates have discovered.**

2. **We give you an inside look into the different types of interview styles you might encounter and how to approach and conquer them.**

3. **We give you guidance from a philosophical point of view when it comes to deciding what job is right for you.**

This is a practical guide that simplifies the process, eliminates the unknowns, and explains how to master the essentials.

But first, let us introduce ourselves. Together we have formed a development business, Driven Vision, focused on the mission of helping you "Elevate Your Future." The founders of Driven Vision, as well as the authors of this book, are: Alex Dalpiaz, Hunter Freeman, and Kendall Wernet. We all come from different backgrounds and experiences. We are Generation Y individuals and can relate to the struggles and obstacles facing our generation.

We have been professionally working together for over three years, coaching motivated college students in the field of self development. We decided to capitalize on our knowledge, expand our teachings, and fuel our passion of developing individuals by creating this book to give readers an edge in the career search. We are very passionate about helping people achieve success and measure our own success based on that of others. We devoted a lot of time, effort, and energy into this book, and we hope you find it valuable. Everything discussed in this book is based on personal experience. There is no "fluff" in anything we talk about. We give you specific and precise tips, methods, and actions that can positively affect you and your career search. Everything in this book is advice we have applied to our own lives and endeavors. We have coached individuals using these tips to test our methods and found them to be effective.

Before you read any further, you must decide for yourself that you are willing to be COACHABLE. We define "being coachable" as being able to take information and advice and apply it in an effective fashion as prescribed.

If you are willing to step out of your comfort zone and evolve your current mindset, you are going to benefit the most from this book. If you are closed off to the ideas presented, we fear a lack of success will be your destiny. We hope you truly appreciate this book, gain confidence, and yield success through the information

provided. Enjoy!

WHAT IS YOUR GOAL?
NOT BECOMING PART OF A JOBLESS GENERATION

Before we dive into some helpful information, let's set the stage for you and build in some perspective. If you're reading this book, you have taken a very positive step forward in accomplishing your goal to land a job. Graduation is approaching very quickly, and you now have to put your attention and effort toward your future. If you are like the average college graduate these days, you are graduating with nearly $29,400 worth of debt (as of 2012) with no end in sight, according to *Time Magazine*. That amount will take an average college student (assuming you attain a fulltime job) anywhere from 10-20 years to pay off. In addition, *Time Magazine* also revealed that 11.5% of student loans were delinquent.

Just imagine 10% of your income being instantaneously subtracted from your paycheck to pay back your student loans for the next 15 years of your life. Student loans are debts that you cannot run from and will haunt you forever.

Although student loans provide an otherwise impossible means for many people to attend college from a financial standpoint, they are not just going to disappear. Not to mention by the time you do pay them off, you have paid back nearly twice of what you originally borrowed.

Big numbers and mounting debt are scary to any graduating student, but what we want you to realize is how important it is to allow yourself freedom from these debts and relieve stress by landing a job. College graduates are now having a harder time gaining employment than ever before.

We have been deemed a jobless generation for good reason. Graduating students are underemployed, underpaid, and face a lifetime of financial burdens because of the lack of job market opportunities. It is competition at its finest. Getting a degree is not good enough to translate into a guaranteed job. You have to work for a job. Getting a job is a job all in itself. We want you to gain this perspective because we truly want you to fall in the category of the individuals who DO obtain a position upon graduation. We believe the toughest part is actually *getting the opportunity to interview and exhibit yourself as a qualified candidate for that position.*

Everything you have learned is of little value until you have an opportunity to showcase it to a potential employer. This is why the lessons and advice in this book give you that extra boost you need to put you in front of someone to share your story. As stressful as it may be, it is also a very exciting time for you. This is what all your hard work in school has led up to. You are at the doorstep of a whole new adventure.

CAREER FAIR

One of the most intimidating situations for a job hunter is the moment you walk into a Career Fair. A career fair is an amazing opportunity in which roles are reversed and the employers come to you. The advice and strategies we have collected are steps that less than 1% of people know about and increase your chances of landing that desired job. A career fair is usually your first time in front of an employer, and it can be a valuable opportunity that either makes you or breaks you.

The first thing to keep in mind when attempting to conquer a career fair is to know your audience. In this situation, your audience is the employers attending the event. This is the time when doing significant research on the event itself and the employers will surely pay off. Just about every career fair makes it known ahead of time who will be in attendance, and this can be used to your advantage

If it is a multi-day career fair, make note of which employers are attending which day or days. It's important to know this simple fact as you do not want to miss the opportunity to speak with an employer of choice simply because you attended the wrong day. After you are knowledgeable about the employers attending, it is important for you to prioritize your time and pinpoint which companies you'd most like to meet with. You only have a limited amount of time at a career fair and you do not want to spend time with an employer that does not meet your needs. So what can you do to filter out unwanted employers?

First, research the company itself. There may be several you are not familiar with, so you should begin with identifying basic details for each hiring business. Spending time on the company's website and doing background research is a great way to familiarize yourself with what they have to offer. Some good things to look for are locations of work, what line of work are they in, how long the company has been in existence, who runs the company, their impact on their community, etc.

After spending time looking up the background and finding more about the potential employer, start looking to see if the company is a fit for you based on your education and experiences. Basically, find the employer that has an opening in your desired interest of work.

A useful tip is to spend time checking out the company's "Careers" page on their website. This is usually very easy to find and is often visible from the main page. Look for a link like the following: "Careers," "Work for Us," "Career Opportunities," etc. It's all going to lead you to the same place. The purpose of exploring the company's career page beforehand is to become knowledgeable about the positions they are currently hiring for. You can read into the details of each position and glean valuable insight into the company's expected qualifications and characteristics for a new team member. This is also valuable because most of the time the positions you see listed online are the same positions the recruiters at the career fair are looking to fill. BOOM! You just got one step ahead of everyone else. Use any and all information you find beforehand on the employer's website to your full advantage. Use the worksheet template on the next page to help you keep track of each employer you research.

CAREER FAIR EMPLOYER TRACKER

Employer:

Available Date(s):

Position Available:

Locations:

Facts/Notes:

Questions:

Now you have completed the necessary background research to allow you to fully take advantage of you career fair opportunity. However, the following information will be the single most important key you must master to maximize your hiring potential. After all, your number one goal in reading this book is to produce results, and your results are measured by the job offers you receive. So at this point, your research is complete, but before you actually speak with these employers, you need to master a precise "pitch."

You may have heard it before, but while having a pitch is the most important tool you can use, it is also the most overlooked step by job hunters. Less than 1% of the candidates you are competing against will be using this method. They just do not realize the effectiveness and the importance of properly portraying themselves to an employer. In fact, the pitch we are about to describe is actually what recruiters *want* to hear. By mastering this pitch, you position yourself as a first-round draft pick to take the next step in their hiring process. Hold on, here we go!

Your pitch is going to be what you say when you first approach a recruiter at their "recruiting table" at a career fair. I'm sure you know how important first impressions are! First we will give you the outline to create your own pitch following our outline, and then we'll explain to you how to effectively use it.

In your introduction, you will simply, but positively, state your full name, your class status (Junior, Senior, etc.), and when you will be graduating (spring, summer, of 2015).

"Hi! My name is James Duncan. I am a senior here at Clemson University, graduating this May."

Next, discuss your Major (main educational background) and Minor (or secondary area of study).

"Hi! My name is James Duncan. I am a senior here at Clemson University, graduating May of 2015. I am graduating with a degree in Business Management, with a minor in Communications and a secondary degree focus in Marketing."

At this point, you can begin to watch the eyes of this recruiter grow wide, as you have already grabbed their attention. They will be hanging on to each and every word that you articulate, so let's make sure you make a powerful statement. You are now going to discuss a brief outline of your background, work experience, and some minor details associated with the two. It's best to talk about your most recent and most powerful work history, which has ideally occurred within the past two years. Feel free to discuss whatever you think will gain the most interest from the recruiter. You will also notice several "buzzwords" (such as incredible, unique, utilization) thrown in. These add to the overall effect and can be really beneficial.

"Hi! My name is James Duncan. I am a senior here at Clemson University, graduating this May. I am graduating with a degree in Business Management, a minor in Communications, and a secondary degree focus in Marketing. Over the past two years, I have had an incredible and unique experience interning at BMW. This paid internship allowed me to work alongside the senior leadership team. I worked on various projects, conducted several meetings, and gave countless presentations. One of the most influential projects I participated in was when I lead an employee utilization project to discover the employee utilization percentage on the assembly line. My research yielded some very interesting results."

It's a mouthful, but that's not a bad thing. You have just explained to the recruiter a brief history of your work experience and some specific details on the work you did there. Above was just an example – everyone's pitch will be different. However, you should try to follow this format and insert the details pertaining to you.

Following your introduction is a great opportunity to discuss what you are looking for in a career and what you like most. This is where you speak to your personal preferences and goals.

"Hi! My name is James Duncan. I am a senior here at Clemson University, graduating May of 2015. I am graduating with a degree in Business Management, a minor in Communications, and a secondary degree focus in Marketing. Over the past two years, I have had an incredible and unique experience interning at BMW. This paid internship allowed me to work alongside the senior leadership team there. I worked on various projects, conducted several meetings, and gave countless presentations. One of the most influential projects I participated in was a time I took lead on employee utilization project to find out the utilization percentage of the employees on the assembly line. My research yielded some very interesting results. What I am looking for most in a career is one that provides me the greatest amount of opportunity. I'm looking for a positive work environment where I am rewarded for my effort and contribution to the company. I am looking for an opportunity to grow within the company and achieve new positions and more responsibility."

Now for the final step – this is where doing your

research will pay off. It will show the recruiter you took time to research what their company is all about and the type of work they do. You may want to refer to an open position you are aware of or some basic attributes of the company you admire.

"Hi! My name is James Duncan. I am a senior here at Clemson University, graduating May of 2015. I am graduating with a degree in Business Management, a minor in Communications, and a secondary degree focus in Marketing. Over the past two years, I have had an incredible and unique experience interning at BMW. This paid internship allowed me to work alongside the senior leadership team there. I worked on various projects, conducted several meetings, and gave countless presentations. One of the most influential projects I participated in was a time I took lead on employee utilization project to find out the utilization

percentage of the employees on the assembly line. My research yielded some very interesting results. What I am looking for most in a career, is one that provides me the greatest opportunity. I'm looking for a positive work environment where I am rewarded for my effort and contribution to the company. I am looking for an opportunity to grow within the company and achieve new positions and more responsibility. In doing some earlier research, I noticed that your company has a strong Manager in Training position that I am extremely interested in. I believe it would be a perfect opportunity for me and your company."

Execute this correctly and the recruiter will want to interview you on the spot. Good news for you, right? Absolutely!

After reading the sample pitch, you are probably feeling one of two emotions. The first emotion is one of excitement and desire to actually use this. You are probably someone who is not necessarily afraid of career fairs, but more of someone who just didn't know how to fully take advantage of them. You now have some really great information to lead yourself in the right direction.

If you are in the second group of people, your emotions are probably causing you to feel overwhelmed, nervous, or intimidated. Those are absolutely normal emotions. After all, if this technique came naturally to everyone, there would be no need for this section of the book – everyone would be using it.

When it's all said and done, your pitch will probably last around 30-45 seconds. Do not let it last any longer than that to prevent unnecessary rambling and to avoid the risk of a recruiter losing interest.

PRACTICE, PRACTICE, PRACTICE your pitch many times before presenting it to a recruiter. You should not have any problems remembering it, but make sure it sounds genuine! Don't be robotic!

ENVIRONMENT OF A CAREER FAIR

As we touched on earlier, going to a career fair can be overwhelming because it is looked at as a pinnacle moment in your life. All your schooling, education, and work experience is coming down to how well you perform at a career fair. It's like a professional baseball player trying to earn his way into the Hall of Fame by the outcome of just one swing of the bat.

To put you at ease, you should not look at a career fair with such esteem. It is not a matter of life or death. A career fair is simply an opportunity to speak with employers. We are not trying to say that you shouldn't capitalize fully on this opportunity; we're just providing a reminder that the sun will still come up tomorrow, regardless of the interview outcome.

Most of the stress from a career fair, like we mentioned earlier, comes from being unprepared. "Be Prepared" is the Boy Scout motto for a reason! When you are prepared, you statistically always perform better. After all, if you fully prepare for a big test, you are more confident that you are going to do well than if you had not studied at all.

Part of preparing for the career fair is understanding the environment you will be walking into (literally). If you have been to any sort of a career fair before, you may recall how intimidating it was to enter an unfamiliar environment. Whether this is your first career fair or you're a well-seasoned attendant, it will help to be knowledgeable about the venue. After all, the more you know, the more comfortable you are.

When walking into a career fair, you can expect to be greeted by a friendly staff member who will sign you in or register you in some way. This should be a very brief encounter with a goal to gain some of your basic information.

At this point, it is time to get down to business and you are probably already feeling your heartbeat rise as you see the dozens of employers ahead of you. You will most likely be in a gym, hotel lobby, sport venue, etc. It really makes no difference. It's time to make it your territory. Become familiar with your venue, gather your nerves, look over your pitch and notes one last time, and scout out where the employers you want to connect with are located.

Take about 5-7 minutes and simply walk around your career fair. Take a lap. Pay attention to the booths and where the employers are lined up. You should be referring to your list of predefined employers that you plan to speak with. Locating each employer beforehand will allow you to solely focus on your interactions with potential employers and showcasing your talent. Doing this is kind of like stretching your muscles before you go on a run.

Upon learning the location of the employers that

you plan to speak with first, you are now ready to initiate your first conversation.

One tip that we would like for you to take into account here is to give your first pitch to an employer you are not interested in. Basically, think of this like a scrimmage. This is great opportunity to give your pitch to someone that you are not concerned with. It is a great time to get your final practice in, get the jitters out, and if you mess up, it's not that big of a deal. By doing a "practice pitch," you will feel much more comfortable when you are speaking with the employers you are actually interested in, and you will perform much better. At this point, you are free to speak with your employers of choice. Have at it!

WHAT TO BRING WITH YOU

There are many things in the recruiting process that you cannot control. However, one of the things you can control 100% are the things that you bring with you to the career fair. There are few mandatory items we require anyone to bring with them. Use your best judgment and creativity for any additional items.

The first and most important item is your resume. This is not a book about how to write a resume, nor is it intended to be one. You should absolutely seek out professional help and guidance when formatting and putting together your resume. Take the time to have someone help you construct a resume that is to a professional standard. There are many resources out there to help you do that.

The reason we want you to seek out professional help is because recruiters take them very seriously. We have heard countless stories of recruiters not getting past a candidate's name on a resume before throwing it in the trash because it was not formatted correctly and to a professional standard. Do not lose out on an opportunity because you didn't take the time to sharpen your resume. Make sure to proofread it, too!

Print out several copies, more than you think you will need. If you plan to talk to 10 employers that day, print out 20. You'll want to have extra copies on hand in case you strike up a conversation with someone unexpected.

Next, you want to have a padfolio to keep everything organized. A padfolio is a portable case that opens like a book to reveal a notepad. Its primary function is to keep your documents accessible and organized. They are inexpensive and can easily be picked up at any office supply store. We recommend having a padfolio because it makes you look professional. It gives you something to hold all your resumes and keep your notes organized while you are speaking with recruiters. If you do not have one, go get one!

Next, make sure you bring your personal and employer background notes and keep them handy for the entirety of the career fair. It is to your benefit to bring all your background notes along so you can easily refer to them whenever you want. Finally, make sure to have two pens just in case one pen breaks or is misplaced. This will allow you to take notes or write down contact information when meeting a potential employer.

One thing that we want to quickly cover is how to dress for a career fair. As we started thinking about all the people we have seen dress inappropriately for career fairs, we decided this part was essential. Everyone knows the cliché sayings, "Dress Your Best" and "Dress for the job you want, not the job you have." Well, they are never truer than here.

Anytime you will be interacting with potential employers, always dress in your Sunday best. Men should have on a suit or a jacket and tie. Women should wear dress slacks or a knee-length skirt with a professional blazer, or a suit. If you do not have access to an outfit of that standard, find a friend and borrow a suit. We have seen so many guys go to career fairs wearing khaki pants and a tucked in polo shirt or a tucked in button up. We understand that it takes slightly more bit of effort to dress up, but making a visual impression to recruiters is very important. Ladies, be conservative with your outfit and do not be too revealing. Remember, you are attempting to present yourself as a professional adult, so you need to dress like it. You will not be taken seriously by a recruiter if you are not dressed professionally.

Recruiters will instantly pass you over as a candidate if you do not have on professional attire. In other words, don't even waste your time going to a career fair if you are not going to be dressed professionally.

TYPICAL RECRUITER ENCOUNTERS AND THE APPROACH

One of our primary goals is to prepare you for communicating your pitch during your first recruiter encounter. We want you to be prepared for any possibilities, and by considering these situations beforehand, they are less likely to throw you off in the moment.

When approaching a company's booth, you may have to wait in line a few minutes while other applicants are speaking with the recruiter. This is normal and shouldn't be anything for you to worry about. Just wait patiently and be ready for your turn.

Another inside tip we want to throw your way at this point is to be very observant of the recruiter(s). At most career fairs, there are usually two recruiters from the same company at each booth. This simply speeds up the process and prevents one from being overwhelmed. Be observant to determine the "dominant" or "head" recruiter. This may not be obvious, but usually if there are two individuals, one will be a prominent and tenured recruiter, while the other is most likely a recent graduate or a recruiter-in-training. This is not to say you should think any less of a new recruiter, but you are more likely to stand a better chance of taking the next step by speaking to the head recruiter. He or she is more likely to be appreciative and impressed by your pitch and quickly recognize you as a serious candidate. Consider if this person speaks very clearly about the company, explains things well, is very focused and direct, and exudes authority and confidence like a head recruiter.

When you approach the recruiter, make sure to greet them with a warm smile. Your body language indirectly communicates to a recruiter, so make sure you approach the situation with confidence.

Remember, you are one of several dozen, if not hundreds, of people this recruiter will be speaking with throughout the day, so you want to be memorable. Your amount of preparation should allow this moment to occur naturally and professionally. As you approach, greet the recruiter with a warm, "Hello, my name is Sara, how are you today?" As you are doing this, reach out to shake the recruiter's hand.

The recruiter will most likely respond back with a simple, yet friendly, "Hello, Sara, my name is Dave. I am doing well today." At this point, it is imperative that you maintain control of the situation by filling the open opportunity with your pitch. Believe it or not, the recruiter is actually expecting you to begin the conversation and take initiative at this point. That's why jumping into your pitch and telling your story is the perfect direction to take. While your tendency may be to allow the recruiter to speak first, your initiative will display your leadership qualities and confidence.

NEXT STEPS AFTER THE PITCH ENDS

At this point, the hardest part is over with and you've done your task. You have just completed your introduction and pitch to the recruiter and are awaiting the next steps. What happens next can go in several directions, and it really depends on the recruiter and their career fair style. We will give you a few possible scenarios and some valuable tips to help take things in a positive direction.

When you finish your pitch, the first thing you will probably notice is an increased interest from the recruiter. At this point, the recruiter has been having pointless, lifeless conversations with dozens of applicants, and you are going to be a much needed breath of fresh air. The recruiter will likely ask for your resume. Certainly! Boom, you have your padfolio handy with your resume all ready to go to distribute.

The recruiter will begin asking follow-up questions gleaned either from your resume or pitch. The questions will be simple and straightforward. Do not stress too much about them. The more questions and conversations that occur between the two of you, the better. Recruiters usually show their cards of how interested they are in you by the amount of questions they ask. This is not always the case, but you should feel hopeful if many questions are asked.

At this point, the two of you will exchange some light conversations and the recruiter will most likely go into detail about the company, the type of candidates they are looking for, and the open positions. A typical question asked is, "Where would you like to live?" or something like, "We are only looking to fill positions for our Denver office, would that work for you?"

The first word without hesitation out of your mouth should always be "Absolutely, I have no geo-graphical limitations." Even if at that current time you are not completely sure about geographical restrictions for yourself, you should never let the recruiter know that.

You never want to discuss money or geography with a recruiter until you have a written offer from the company. It is at that point you have leverage and can begin negotiations. Until then, approach each employer with an open mindset. Basically, do not let the recruiters know there are any factors that would keep you from working for them.

It is also good practice to throw the ball back to the recruiter and show your interest by asking a few follow-up questions. The conversation can go in several directions, depending on the circumstances and the individual recruiter's process. This is another situation in which being aggressive will pay off.

The number one thing on your mind at this point should be to know the next steps in the company's hiring or recruiting process. Most recruiters will explain it to you, but if they don't or do not explain it in detail, feel free to ask. A good way of phrasing it would be to say something like: "I appreciate your time today, Tim, and if you do not mind, I'd like to understand more about the next steps you will be taking after this career fair regarding the hiring process." Your goal is to find out the next steps the recruiter will be taking once he/she finds candidates from the career fair.

It is very important for you to know this. Why? Because it keeps you in tune with how the recruiter will be operating. Here are the things you are trying to figure out:

- When will the recruiter be letting candidates they meet at the career fair know if they qualify for the next steps in the hiring process?

- What are the next steps in the hiring process?

- When are the interviews?

- Who will be conducting the interviews?

- Where will the interviews be taking place?

Questions like these allow you to know what to expect next. Some recruiters will let candidates know on the spot if they qualify as someone they want to take the next steps with. Most recruiters will let you know they are going to be looking over all the candidates and resumes that evening and they will be calling all qualified candidates the next day to set up interviews. This will be the typical response and should be taken positively.

When wrapping things up with the recruiter, make sure to record their contact information. They usually will give you their business card with all their information. We also recommend taking any handouts and materials on the company displayed at their booth. This will give you some extra ammunition for when you go to the interview. When your time with that recruiter is running out and you have accomplished your mission, verbally let the recruiter know that you are "very interested in the position and taking the next steps in the hiring process." You are just simply confirming that you want an opportunity to interview for the job. Genuinely thank the recruiter for their time and shake their hand. Your encounter with that company is now 95% over with. Yes, even though you have hopefully blown them away, you still have one final step to take.

Remember how we mentioned about taking the information of the recruiter with you? Well, now is the time to use it to your advantage. That evening when you go home, turn on your computer and log into your email. To seal the deal with a cherry on top, write the recruiter a very short email thanking them once again for their time today. It should go something like this:

To: bobjones@bestbuy.com

From: PeterFreeman@yahoo.com

Subject: Peter Freeman-University of Florida-Thank You

Mr. Jones,

Thank you so much for your time today at the career fair. I really enjoyed the time getting to talk with you and learn more about the great opportunities that Best Buy has to offer. I sincerely hope you will consider me as a candidate to interview for (a specific position). I really believe that I could contribute to Best Buy's vision as an industry leader in home electronics. I also attached my resume for you for convenience.

Have a great day,

Peter Freeman

peterfreeman@yahoo.com

869.888.8765

Once you have done this, your mission is now 100% complete. You have done everything possible to maximize your opportunity to get an interview. You now have the tools to conquer any career fair with confidence and aggression.

INTERVIEWS

Interviews are designed, exist, or intended for two reasons. The first is to help you decide if you want to work for the potential company, and the second is to help the employer to determine if you would be a good fit for the company. Interviewing is by far one of the most important parts in the process of acquiring a job. Although several people are afraid of interviews, you do not need to be. If you just take the time to prepare for your interview, it is nothing to be afraid of.

Pre-Interview Tips

Research the Company

Remember all the research that you did on companies for the career fair? It is going to come in handy again for your interview. Before you interview, gather all the information you can about the company, recruiter(s), and the position that you are interviewing for. The more information you begin with, the better off you will be in your interview.

Info About Recruiters

One major thing to note about an interview is the process begins as soon as you first make contact with the recruiter, whether that is on the phone, in person, or by email. At that moment, the recruiter immediately forms thoughts about you and starts to analyze both you and your potential.

Recruiters will analyze everything about you, so it is vital that you make an exceptional first impression because there is not a second chance to do so. The recruiter will be listening to you speak and reading your resume, so it is important that you are genuine and professional.

Recruiters can immediately tell if you are not prepared so be on point and do your research.

Dress

If you are meeting for your interview in person, you want to make sure that you are dressed the part. It is always better to be overdressed rather than underdressed.

Things to Bring

For every interview, you should always bring a few essentials with you. You will want to make sure you bring a hard copy of your resume. Bring two more copies than you think you need, just in case there are any extra recruiters at the interview that you were not expecting. This ensures any recruiters present do not have to pass your resume around. It also portrays you as someone that thinks ahead, a trait high sought after, since you will be very well prepared for the unexpected – scoring you some points early on.

Along with your resume, you will also want to bring two pens, yes two. Having two pens will also show that you think ahead, but most importantly ensure that you have something to write your notes down with should something happen to your first pen.

The next essential item to bring along is a notepad. A padfolio is highly recommended and a great investment if you do not have one. Whatever you do, don't bring a scrap piece of paper or a notepad that looks terrible. You need to maintain a professional appearance across everything you do. Also, make sure your paper is lined to help keep everything organized.

Tips During an Interview

Body Language

Body language is an extremely important aspect of an interview and it is often overlooked. When interviewing, make sure to maintain eye contact whenever possible. Eye contact increases the level of trust and helps increase retention and comprehension.

Do not tap your feet or fingers and definitely make sure not to click or tap your pen. These little fidgeting movements show you are nervous or bored, and you definitely do not want your recruiter to think that you are either of those.

Make sure you never cross your arms. Crossing your arms portrays vulnerability and lower status. You want to appear strong and have the ability to take command.

Questions

When preparing for an interview, recruiters will take time to carefully design their questions

Questions will be targeted toward various aspects depending on the position and company you are interviewing for. They will generally seem to be broad, but just know there is a purpose for asking it.

The questions will almost always be open-ended, requiring you to respond with an answer more than just a simple response or a yes or no. They want you to talk about your answer, not just answer their question. They design the questions to be broad in order to see how you respond.

Responding

Responding to questions during an interview is generally the most daunting task, but it does not need to be. While your response to the questions is essential to your interview, by following a few simple rules you can make your responses very powerful.

During interviews, and in every professional interaction for that matter, it is important to know when to talk. You do not want to cut someone off who is just pausing. The best and easiest way to do avoid doing so is by using the two second rule. The two second rule is simple as all you need to do is count to two in your head after the person stops talking and before you respond. This rule is incredibly useful not only on the phone, but in person as well.

During an interview, it is extremely important to remember the 60/40 rule. You want to do 60 percent of the talking, while your recruiter does 40 percent. When followed, this will ensure that you do not speak too much or too little. Although the 60/40 rule is the primary time rule that should be followed, it can often be hard to judge your responses based upon it.

To better assess the time variable for each individual response, try using the rule of twos.

The first two is applied to your pause after the question is asked and before you respond. During an interview it is crucial you take your time to really think about the question being answered. It can be a good idea to actually pause and take a few seconds to think about the question. Now it's important to not make this pause too long, so a good rule of thumb is to count to two in your head before responding.

It can be very hard to actually know how long you should take for your response. That is why the second two is applied to your response itself. To know how long your individual responses should be, use the two minute rule. Your goal with this rule is to keep your response as close to two minutes in length as possible. This will ensure two things: that your recruiter will not get bored or sidetracked, and it will also ensure that you know how much information is needed for a solid response. Be sure to use your best judgment on response length, as some questions may only require a 20 second response. In these cases, you will make an exception to the rule as there is no sense if filling your response with unnecessary fluff just to make it two minutes long.

A good response itself is not hard to form. There are many different ways to go about responding to questions, but there are a few response types that are most common. One response example starts with the straightforward answer that is short, to the point, and answers the question being asked. Now as we said, you do not want to do just this, so in this case you would want to immediately elaborate on your answer. When elaborating, be sure to explain the reason behind why you believe that your answer is so. You want to provide details and facts if possible. Bringing up a situation or experience that you have been through is a great way to explain your answer.

Another great way to answer a question in an interview is by telling a story relevant to the question. After the question is asked, take your two seconds to think about your answer then transition to the story. A great way to transition is by simply telling the recruiter you will be telling them a story. This lets them know what is going on and helps them understand.

When telling a story in an interview, it is very important that you do not include unnecessary components and do not drag it on, or the recruiter could get annoyed or not understand the point you are trying to convey. Once the story is told, make sure to summarize it quickly by stating how it answers the question that was being asked. Stories are great for answering questions where the recruiter ask you to tell them about something.

Notes

If you think of questions that you have during your interview, jot them down on your notepad. One way to quickly do this is to simply write a word or two that will help you remember your question, rather that writing the full question out. Circle the note on your pad to ensure you can easily find it among your other notes. This will allow you to continue to pay attention to your recruiter or continue talking yourself. Once your recruiter is done asking questions, you can read back through your notes and remember your questions.

Types of Interviews

One on One

In a one on one interview, you are sitting across from your recruiter and they are simply asking you a wide range of questions. It is a very simple interview that does not generally require much more than responding to the questions being asked.

As your one on one interview winds up and before you leave, make sure to ask your recruiter for a business card if you do not already have one. If your recruiter did not tell you when they would follow up or when you should follow up with them, be sure to set a date to do so and write this down. Do not forget to shake hands with your recruiter and thank them for their time and the opportunity to interview with their company.

Group Interview

There are two types of group interviews: one being a panel group and the other a candidate group

Panel Group

Panel interviews always scare people, but after you understand a little bit about them and their purpose, you can ace them.

A panel interview is when there is a team of recruiters interviewing you. Panels are strategically compiled of select individuals within the company. The members are usually those that have expertise from different departments within the business. Some common positions that members will hold within the company are hiring manager, human resources manager, or technical manager. These individuals will generally be asking questions related to their department and expertise to better help them assess your fit.

Equal

Although each member is there for a reason, they are all working toward a common goal. It is important that you do not favor any of them and be sure to treat each member as an equal.

Be sure to stay engaged with the panel, so if they laugh, laugh along. Engage each individual. Smile and talk to all of them, not just the person asking the question. Also be sure to have questions for the panel at the end. It is best to have a separate question for each member, if possible.

When walking into a panel interview, if given the chance, be sure to shake all the members' hands. As you do so, introduce yourself to each of them individually and gather business cards from each person, if they have one. Carefully stack the business cards on top of each other in order the members are sitting. When you get to your seat, lay the business cards out in front of you. This will allow you to remember all of their names and so you can address them properly. If they do not have a card, simply write their name down on a piece of paper or the back of one of your cards and place it in the correct spot.

Questions

With a panel interview, you can expect to get questions from multiple members. Each member will usually form their own set of questions. This can become tricky, since everyone has their own style of wording and asking questions. It is important to take each member individually as to not feel over-whelmed. You will have to pay extra close attention to the question being answered and be sure you answer it.

When leaving a panel interview, you should thank each member and shake everyone's hand. Since you gathered everyone's card or name, you can easily follow up and thank each member individually.

Candidate Group

Candidate group interviews consist of a group of interviewees, like you, that are all interviewing at the same time in the same room for the same position.

When waiting for your candidate interview to start, do not sit silently, on your phone, or look at your notebook. Look around and try to figure out who the other candidates are, introduce yourself, and start talking to them. Get their name and write it down on your notepad. Ask them questions and get to know them a little, as this will help increase interaction during the interview and put you in a better position.

During candidate interviews, you may be asked questions or asked to complete a task or activity. If questions are being asked, the recruiter may direct them to individuals separately or ask the group as a whole. Recruiters may ask different questions to each person, so be ready.

When you are interacting with the other candidates, make sure to use their name as it will display you as a leader and help you stand out. If you are responding to a question, you can also refer to the other candidates by name by saying something like, "Kendall and I were just talking about..." When other candidates are talking, be sure to listen carefully and if you can, build off of what they were saying. Give praise and let the other candidates know you appreciate their ideas. This is as easy as saying, "Alex that is a great idea..." It will display authority and leadership.

Another thing to remember for candidate interviews is the importance of balance. You need to make sure you are not too loud, but also not too shy. Don't let yourself get bullied by the other candidates and remain quiet. You want to do your best to dominate the conversation, but do not overpower others and make sure to give everyone a chance to talk. Be confident and encourage your fellow interviewees to participate and to speak up. If someone is being shy or quiet, address them directly by their name and ask them a question or for their opinion.

When the interview is over, do not just thank and shake hands with your recruiter. Be sure to acknowledge your fellow candidates as well.

Phone Interview

Phone interviews are generally the least stressful type of interview because you do not have to sit directly in front of your recruiter. Although you are not directly in the presence of your recruiter, it is very important that you do not forget that it is still an interview. It can become easy to forget and you do not want to stop being professional or let your guard down just because your recruiter is not present.

You can do a few simple things that will ensure you are on point and stay focused during the interview. Some of these may seem odd at first, but I promise they have been proven to work. One tactic recommended is to dress as though you were leaving to go to an interview. Just because you are not actually meeting face to face does not mean you cannot dress up. Dressing for an interview will ensure that you feel like you are in an interview and help you maintain your professionalism throughout.

Another thing you will want to do while on the phone is walk around and smile – no joke. Walking around increases blood flow throughout your body, thus keeping you alert and increasing the energy of your voice. Smiling will increase your happiness and directly affect your tone. Being on the phone means that whoever is on the other end cannot see you, so all they have to go by are your words and tone.

It is vital that you have a very clear and strong connection. Make sure you are not driving as you never know if a call could drop.

Meal Interview

Meal interviews can seem easy, but it is important to not get complacent and too comfortable.

Before the interview, make sure you get a copy of

the menu. Many restaurants have them online and if they do not you can often call and have one emailed over to you. Once you have the menu, pick out exactly what you want to order. Pre-planning what you will order will save you a lot of trouble when at the table with your recruiter.

Make sure to arrive early and try to be the first one there. Even though you arrive early, be sure to check with the hostess to make sure that your party has not already arrived. If you are the first one there, make sure to wait in the lobby and not at the bar.

When ordering a drink don't get anything alcoholic or any pop. Stick to something professional like water, sparkling water, or iced tea. Remember, no matter what, do not drink out of a bottle or a straw.

Make sure to order something small that is not messy or smelly and that can be eaten with a fork and knife. Also, make sure not to order the most expensive or the cheapest thing. Do not order messy sandwiches or burgers, and do not change how your order comes. If something is wrong with your food, do not say anything just eat it and move on.

Make sure you do eat something, and whatever you order, eat at least half of it. No matter what do not get a to go box. Only order dessert if the interviewer does, and kindly accept the interviewer's offer to pay, you were their guest after all.

What is nice about an interview over a meal is that you can think about your answer to their questions while you are chewing. This will give you more time to develop your best answer possible.

SELECTING A JOB

Money vs. Happiness

Throughout your life, there are essentially two strong factors that determine whether or not you continue with the same job. However, sometimes one will outweigh the other, thus making the other no longer noteworthy. These two factors are money and happiness.

When offered a job, this is where you want to say "SHOW ME THE MONEY!" The single most important piece of information to you is how much money you will be earning so that you can actually live and thrive like any other person in this penny-pinching country. Ask yourself, though: "Would

I rather earn more money or be happier at my workplace?" Your answer may be different depending on where you are in life. For example, if you have just graduated grad school, have thousands of dollars in student loans to pay off, and your wife has your third kid on the way, then the money might seem like an absolute must!

Money trumps all. This is how society has cultured us to think. If we see a dollar bill on the ground, we pick it up. A dollar bill feels good to hold in your hand and even better when it has Benjamin Franklin on the front. Money represents the freedom to buy whatever you want whenever you want it.

Or just by saving up money, it represents security. A millionaire is more likely to invest in a risky stock than a middle-class man or woman. The millionaire can lose some money and still be okay.

So, going back to our original question: "More money or more happiness?" Well, to make this more cut and dry, we are going to define "happiness at your workplace."

Ask yourself these questions about your job. (If you do not currently have a job, great! You are a clean slate and we want to help pick the perfect one.)

- Are you excited to go to work every day?

- Do you enjoy whom you work with?

- Are you friends with your co-workers?

- Is the weekend always the best part of your week?

- Do you respect and listen to your boss/executive?

And, the most important question we want you to ask yourself is:

- If you were offered a job doing the same thing at a different company for $1,000 a year, would you leave your job?

If you answer yes, then you are probably not happy in your current situation.

These questions are simple, but hopefully they got you thinking about how you actually feel about your job, taking money out of the equation. Answering these questions will start you off on a good path to understanding the benefits of choosing a job for money versus choosing a job for happiness.

Is happiness overrated or is money overrated?

Now to shift gears, we want you to ask yourself what you are good at. What are you REALLY good at? If you could pick three skills you are a master at, or even close, what would those be? One of the reasons that you are good at these skills is most likely because you also enjoy doing them.

For example, I would argue that a rock star gifted at playing the electric guitar rarely dislikes performing and playing the guitar.

Simply put: you are good at it, so you want to do it.

Instead of thinking along the lines of money versus happiness, perhaps it is better to think: "which job will engage one of my top three skills?" As soon as you find a job that does this…

You will be good at your job.

You will be paid for what you are good at.

Because this is one of your top three skills, you also enjoy it.

This seems quite simple, but it makes sense! Why would you try to do something that's not your best? Yes, the job market can be brutal nowadays, but if you can fully apply yourself to what you are good at, you will be…wait for it…HAPPY.

So are we saying that happiness trumps money in this job selection process?

The choice is up to you. We want to help you make that choice. We will start by weighing the reasons why each side of the spectrum should be considered. Let's start with money.

CHOOSING YOUR JOB FOR MONEY, NOT FOR HAPPINESS

Having a lot of money is good. That's a statement that is difficult to dispute. When it comes to your first job, you may be happy to get simply one job offer and you are forced to take that route. Hey, you have to start somewhere. Ideally, you've used your career fair and interviewing skills to land yourself multiple job offers, and you have the luxury of deciding between some of your favorite companies.

When those initial offers come in, they could possibly include benefits, vacation time, and so forth. All of these are very important things to consider, but for the sake of our comparison, we will use money as the sole representation of what a job has to offer. Compensation. Salary. Cha-Ching. Call it what you want.

Jumping back to something mentioned earlier, a great point to bring up here is that you need to assess your current circumstance. Money can be a huge help if you are in debt or a tough spot. This is a reason to take the job offering more money. You must weigh the options and assess if you can actually take the risk with the "happy" job that pays less. If you are in a tough spot, you most likely will take the "money" job. Live in the present and be realistic.

What is your fantasy? This is the perfect time (yes, right now) to picture what that happy job is. Now bring it back to reality. If that fantasy job were plopped in the real world, how would it pay? The harsh reality is that even though you may have the drive, the passion, and the motivation to pursue your dream job, the money just may not be there. There are many professions that seem like a dream job, but leave you financially crippled.

When considering which job to pick, don't get too

caught up in your fantasy lifestyle where you will get paid to watch movies or taste food. (To those out there that have those jobs, many envy you.)

Not long ago, I met a minor league baseball player who chose to pursue his dream of playing baseball at a professional level. It was not until I conversed with him that I realized what a harsh lifestyle he lived. Barely making enough to get by, a minor league baseball player puts in countless hours every week during the season. He also is required to constantly travel for away games. If he is promoted to a higher level in minor league (there are actually six_levels of minor league baseball before reaching the major league), he must move locations all together.

I then asked him: "So what do you do in the off-season?"

"I wash cars," he said.

"The team doesn't pay you in the offseason?" I replied.

"I wish."

I give major credit to this guy and to any guy who wants to pursue their dream this badly. Being bold and taking risks is highly admirable, but this baseball story really puts an exclamation point on an important main point:

Your passion can become hell

when it becomes a job

As glamorous as television can make some jobs look, in reality, they may not actually be your passion. That is why it is so important to not get too caught up in your fantasy lifestyle. Keep your eyes open in the present, and be smart about which jobs you choose. Glance at your fantasy to make sure you are headed in the right direction.

As we continue to argue the case for the side that is "Pro-Money," there are plenty of realities to point out to you. To break down the world into "how people make a living" is simple.

There are things to be done, and we need the right people to do them.

Read that again.

<u>There are things to be done, and we need the *right* people to do them.</u>

When it comes to any job, there is a certain skill set needed for that job. Skills are valuable in this world! With that said, there are some skills that you can find in almost any person you see as you walk down the street.

Examples include burger flipping, table bussing, floor mopping, etc.

If you work one of these jobs, awesome. Make sure it is either

1. Your Passion, or

2. Providing you the money you need to live.

So, referring back to our original question, are *you* the *right* person for the job you want? With so many jobs out there, some of the highest paying jobs can be correlated with those that need the most skill. What we are recommending as a possible path for choosing a job based on its money return, is seeking out a job that needs a specific skill and then developing the necessary skills to fit that job.

Instead of making the rest of the puzzle fit to your piece, make your piece fit into the puzzle.

Maybe right now your "piece" does not fit because you need to finish college or take on an internship that will give you valuable experience. However, once you start to enhance yourself and learn new skill sets, you will find that your piece can fit into many puzzles!

There are many risks and investments you must take in life, and enhancing yourself is one of them. Putting in the time now to maximize your abilities will pay dividends later. Making yourself fit into a job that can provide you with plenty of cash flow will help you build capital that you can spend however you would like.

Not to mention there are plenty of things that will always have to be paid for such as healthcare and other bills. If you have a family, be prepared to share the wealth. You must also save for your future – never forget about taking care of "Future You." He/she wants to have a good life, too!

Do you feel like you are pro-money? Does the idea of developing yourself for a moneymaking job interest you? You are not alone! Taking a job for money is by no means a bad move. In fact, it can be a very smart move, given the circumstances.

You did not forget about your own happiness though, right? There are still two sides to this equation that needs to be balanced out.

With that said, let's look into finding your dream job.

CHOOSING A JOB FOR HAPPINESS

"When you do what you love, and love what you do, you'll have success, your whole life through."

– Greg S. Reid

Let's throw you into another scenario – you did your homework, you got the interviews, you NAILED the interviews, and now you are looking at two beautiful job offers laid out for you on a silver platter.

Job Offer #1:

Desk job. You will be on the computer 90% of the day. Work environment is chaotic. You work 9-5 p.m., five days a week. (If this sounds like the perfect job for you, which it might, imagine it's something you hate.)

Starting Salary: $60,000

Job Offer #2:

Dream job. Team culture is incredible at the workplace. This is a company you have wanted to work ever since you first met the organization's leaders. This job will surely make you happy. The opportunity to grow is unlimited.

Starting Salary: $40,000

Alright, so time to make a decision. Which do you choose?

Let's break it down. You have two options: one that screams, "I am no fun, but I will pay you well!" and one that shouts, "I am your dream job, but you are going to be struggling with money!"

In this section, we will talk to about why you should 100% choose the *DREAM JOB*. As mentioned earlier, our society is obsessed with money!

We cannot get enough of the stuff! But, what truly matters in your life is happiness. I am talking about true, genuine happiness where you literally just feel good inside.

Happiness comes from being surrounded by positive people – people who are great influences on you, which will enhance your life. Happiness is when you feel comfortable where you are and can be yourself. These ideas need to translate to the workplace.

Your dream job should be somewhere where you feel that you are a valuable part of a family of workers. You should feel that every day is rewarding and enhancing you as a person. Being in a thriving workplace is like a seed sitting in soil, getting all the water, fertilizer, and sunlight that it needs to grow. This is why one of the fantastic things about choosing a job that makes you happy is that there are better opportunities for development.

BE A LIFELONG LEARNER

Never stop learning and you can develop far beyond what you currently believe you can do. Do not fear success and do not fear greatness!

Any job can teach you skills, but a "happy job" (that's what we will call it) increases the chance of development tenfold! If you are passionate about what you are doing for a living, you will be interested in how you can be better at what you do. This will increase your chances of being more innovative, creative, and positive! You will want to see the company, your peers, and yourself succeed.

Honestly, you would be doing yourself a disservice by choosing a job that does not allow personal growth. You have much more potential than you realize, so it is crucial to pick the job that will unleash your maximum potential. Many times, a job may seem intimidating to take on because it is something you love, but you are afraid of turning it into your career. Taking on that challenge could just be the best thing that has ever happened to you. Turning your passion into a job can drive you to perform at a higher level on a daily basis. It can also help you realize that you are one of the best at what you do.

We believe other things start to open up when you do what you want to do. Whether it is through someone you work with, or through yourself, more doors open up when you are in a positive environment you are thriving in!

Now hold up. We know what you are thinking. "Didn't you guys mention earlier how your passion can become hell if it's your job?"

You caught us.

The truth is, it could easily become hell, but it also has the opportunity to be heaven on earth. If your passion has a "happy job" opportunity, and there are signs of potential development, you should take it. Once you take that job, there are two things that could happen – both of which will benefit you!

1. You realize your new job is a perfect fit, and you will continue to grow and prosper there.

2. You realize your passion has become hell! Either you are not as passionate as you thought you were, or it is just better off to keep it a non-paid passion.

Between these two situations, you cannot lose. Do not have any regrets about wishing you had taken one job over the other. Be willing to take that risk so you can live your life without any uncertainty, or "I wish I hads."

There was a recent study that found that 73% of Americans do not enjoy or get fulfillment their jobs on a daily basis. Do you really want to fall into that category? You spend a third of your life working, you should probably enjoy it.

Going back to development, it is crucial that you realize the importance of self-development – especially in jobs where you are wishing the pay was a little higher.

Developing yourself and taking on higher roles in your dream job is the key to making a larger amount of money. Yes, I am bringing money into this argument because you still need to be smart. As soon as you choose to go down the route of your dream job, your debt, bills, and expenses will follow you down that very same route. Set yourself up for success by choosing a job that gives you a future. Ideally, you are in a position where you will eventually be able to work your way up to the top of a chain of workers and leading at a high level.

Although we could probably write a whole other book on leadership, (if we do, buy a copy) it is important to consider your leadership potential. Forget about whether or not you think you can be a leader. If you are doing something you love and you are doing a fantastic job at it, you have the opportunity to be a leader!

We could list out 1,001 adjectives to describe a leader, but to name a few, a leader is positive, forward-looking, charismatic, and someone you can trust.

Let's create a quick scenario. This is a snapshot of you working at your dream job in 10-15 years.

Your good-looking self has been working at your dream job for years now. You love what you do and every day you come to work excited to see the company and yourself grow. You do your daily activities with a smile on your face.

ENTER NEW GUY

A rookie employee is just now starting to work. He is excited, but nervous – just like you were on your first day. He chose this job because it is his passion

– just like you did.

You have the opportunity to mentor the rookie. In fact, because you love what you do and have such a positive attitude about it, the rookie <u>wants</u> to be mentored by you.

Now it is up to you to take on this leadership responsibility to further develop yourself and to further develop your new mentee!

Taking on a leadership role in the workplace will help you more than you know. By taking the first step as a leader, who knows where the next step will take you? Suddenly, you could be on the path to being a supervisor, top-level executive, or the new CEO!

How do we sum up in one word what the "happy job" has in store for you?

<u>Potential.</u>

Potential is a terrible thing to waste.

THE BEST OF BOTH WORLDS

We have discussed money and we have discussed happiness. But can you have them both?

Of course.

In fact, this is why many millionaires are self-made. They were entrepreneurs who did exactly what they wanted to do. Instead of trying to make the puzzle fit around their piece or have their piece fit into a puzzle, they just made their own puzzle!

According to Fidelity, <u>86%</u> of millionaires are self-made.

That also means 86% of millionaires chose a job for happiness. Surely, those millionaires that started their own business did not start something they did not enjoy!

In addition, who's to say that the 14% that were not self-made millionaires did not select a job for happiness as well? It is definitely possible that a large portion of those millionaires started working for a company they loved, and then they steadily worked their way up the totem pole to find themselves making millions as their career progressed and they developed.

WRAPPING IT UP

So many people today get up, go to work, work their shift, go home, eat dinner, go to bed, and then do the whole thing over again the next day. It is robotic. So many people choose this path to "pay the bills."

So, ponder this thought: at YOUR funeral, what would people say about you in your eulogy? Would you rather them talk about how you "paid the bills" and had a nice car, or how you were a passionate and driven person who did what you loved and was always happy?

You are in control of your life. When it comes to making life-changing decisions in your career path, we hope you are able to use the pages in this book as a guide. Remember to always consider your current circumstances, but always think about how you can benefit your future self as well. Using the tools and ideas that we have presented you with will increase your chances of landing that perfect job. The final piece to the puzzle is <u>confidence.</u>

It is crucial to be confident in your decisions. When making any decision at all, you should not be 60% sure. You should either be 110% POSITIVE or 0%. Being confident and bold in your decisions shows that you are dedicated to your choice. You will perform better when you have 110% confidence in your decisions!

Be confident as you embark on a journey at the career fair, set up and perform interviews, and then select your perfect job.

Believe in yourself.

We believe in you.

Now GO! ELEVATE YOUR FUTURE!

Feed Us...With Feedback. Please!

The three of us put a lot of time and energy into this book. Tell us your success stories from the advice provided to you. We would love to feature your story as a reference to other students who may be interested in this book. We live to hear about the success of those we try to help out.

Also, please make sure to check out our leadership website: TheDrivenVision.com. Please subscribe to receive free leadership content. If interested (and super motivated), please contact us about a paid summer internship we have available through our business development company.

If you would like to give us any constructive feedback, we greatly appreciate that, as well. Please email at Feedback@MasteringACareerFair.com us with anything that you think would be helpful to us and development of this book.

Finally, spread the word! If you enjoyed this book and found it helpful, tell your friends on social media.

Go and dominate!

AUTHOR BIOS

Alex Dalpiaz

Growing up in upstate South Carolina, Alex learned early on from his parents to always work hard in life, treat people as you want to be treated, and to challenge the status quo. Alex didn't know he wanted to be an entrepreneur until age 18 when he began an internship with Young Entrepreneurs where he was given an opportunity to run his own business. It was at this point he was bitten by the entrepreneur bug, and he found his calling. He has since coached, developed, and mentored dozens of motivated college students and oversaw the execution of over a million dollars worth of business while still in college.

Alex has since graduated from Clemson University and has taken his passion full time as he continues to grow the company and his passion for success. Alex's determination to help college students succeed is transcribed throughout every page of this book. Enjoy!

Hunter Freeman

Growing up in the west suburbs of Chicago, Hunter was always coming up with business ideas and trying to make money wherever he could. He would always seek out ways he could help others and went out of his way to do so.

Hunter always had entrepreneurial dreams, and while at Clemson University, he got the opportunity to run his own business. He got an internship with Young Entrepreneurs Across America and was able to coach and mentor other college students to run their own businesses. While with Young Entrepreneurs Across America, he oversaw 33% of his division's sales and was on the executive team that created a 50% increase in sales.

Hunter is expanding his coaching within Young Entrepreneurs Across America and also reaching out to help Clemson students with their entrepreneurial dreams. Being able to write this book to share it with others to help them succeed is very exciting to Hunter.

Kendall Wernet

Growing up in the mountains of Asheville, NC, Kendall was always an adventurer. Consistently striving to be well rounded, he pushes his limits to explore the world around him with hopes to always be growing and learning.

At the age of 18, Kendall started college at Clemson University where he started his own painting business with Young Entrepreneurs Across America (YEAA). After his first year, he oversaw a $78,000 business, and by age 20 oversaw businesses that generated over $500,000.

During his time at Clemson, he coached and mentored other college students on how to successfully run their own businesses. He continues to be a leader with YEAA with goals to help many aspiring young entrepreneurs run their first business.

Kendall is beyond excited to share this book with anyone who is targeting a career fair or needs help deciding his or her career path. He not only wants to live life to the fullest, but also wants to help you do the same.

In memory: Sadly, Kendall passed away right before the publication of this book. We have taken it upon ourselves to keep Kendall's hard work alive in the book and make sure that everyone has a chance to read it. He will surely be missed. He loved writing this book, and we hope you enjoy it.

20730412R00062

Made in the USA
San Bernardino, CA
21 April 2015